KIngdom MInds

Richie Sweitzer

yucky papa ink

All My Life

All my life I have had two special loving ladies, both mean the world to me. They helped me get through my childhood. Without them I wouldn't have any seeds planted. That seed was planted at a young age. It was the seed of respect. To this day I have high respect for them. They were always there for me. I will love you very much grandma and great grandma. You will forever be my two special ladies.

By Richie Sweitzer

Blank Space

Sometimes our hearts are like a blank space, full of void and bitterness, walking around with pride in our hearts. Those blank spaces can be healed through the blood of Jesus Christ. My blank spaces were healed by the blood. Your blank spaces can also be healed.

But he was wounded for our transgressions, he was bruised for our iniquities: the chastisement for our peace was upon him; and by his stripes we are healed. (Isaiah 53:5 NKJV)

By Richie Sweitzer

KIngdom MInds

Family Love

Thanksgiving is the best time for family love. The love from family is special. When we should embrace each other with love. Family is what makes the holidays meaningful. This is the time to be thankful. Who do we have! We have our family love. Those who are gone will always be in our heart. Family is a once in a lifetime. Enjoy your family this thanksgiving.

With all lowliness and gentleness, with long suffering, bearing with one another in love, (Ephesians 4:2 NKJV)

By Richie Sweitzer

Bad Blood

We all have a dark side inside of us, that we have locked in us somewhere. You don't want to see my other side. Don't let the smile fool you. My tables can turn quick. So don't mess with me. Everyone has a little bit of bad blood in them. Only use love when needed.

For all have sinned, and come short of the
glory of God, (Romans 3:23 NKJV)

By Richie Sweitzer

Time Travel

Music is like a time machine through the decades. Good music never dies out. Real music legends will always last forever. The name of real music has a reputation. Today's songs puts music to shame. Artists today need to take music lessons; put soul into their music.

By Richie Sweitzer

That Don't Impress Me Much

Some people talk way too much. Others act all spiritual. When reality check you are faking it. Many people talk the talk. That don't impress me much with your lip service. Few people walk the walk. They are giving service with action. So come and repent to Jesus. Don't just have the head, Knowledge.

Put that Knowledge in to action.

He is a double-minded man, unstable in all his ways. (James 1:8 NKJV)

By Richie Sweitzer

Complicated

Sometimes we make things complicated in life. You never know what kind of a ball life will throw at you. We can create our own complications in life. How we respond is what matters. We can respond with Christ like mind set or respond with a natural mind set. For me I choose the Christ like mind set.

Casting all your cares upon him, for he cares for you. (1 Peter 5:7 NKJV)

By Richie Sweitzer

All I Have To Give

This holiday's greatest gift is love to receive. Love is the gift that keeps on giving. She is like a beautiful diamond ring, waiting for someone to put her on. Let's cherish each other with love this Christmas. Without love, there is no Christmas. That love is from Jesus Christ. Merry Christmas everyone.

There let us pursue the things which make for peace and the thing by which one may edify another. (Romans 14:19 NKJV)

By Richie Sweitzer

Health

There are two types of health, spiritual and physical. Your spiritual health is most important. This one gives you the true meaning of life. We must feed or inner man daily. Then comes taking care of the body. The body is the temple of the lord.

For Bodily exercise profits a little, but godliness is profitable for all things, having a promise of the life that now is and that which is to come.

(1 Timothy 4:8 NKJV)

By Richie Sweitzer

New Chapter

With a new year comes a new chapter. Each year that passes is a new chapter in life. Life is like reading a book; the more you read the better it gets. This new year means new adventures to come. More new surprises may come this new year. Love may be in the air for some people this year.

By Richie Sweitzer

Sometimes

Sometimes when you have the pain of hurt. The hurt of childhood scars. My childhood scars still haunt me at times. It's how you respond to the flashback. Don't feel like you're alone with this problem. I am right there with you.

Who comforts us in all our tribulation, that we may be able to comfort those who are in any trouble, with the comfort with which we ourselves are comforted by God. (2 Corinthians 1:4 NKJV)

By Richie Sweitzer

Thankful

This is the time to be thankful for the small things. We should show our gratitude to those we care about. Let our gratitude be shown through love. Thanksgiving is the season to come as one. When we gather to enjoy each other's presence. Family comes in many different forms. These are challenging times this year. Remember the attitude of gratitude. Happy Thanksgiving.

In everything give thanks; for this is the will of God in Christ Jesus for you. (1 Thessalonians 5:18 NKJV)

By Richie Sweitzer

Depression

Depression is a problem today. Many people deal with this issue every day. This is a very real problem. It has grown more this year. Even your favorite poet deals with depression. It makes you want to sleep all day. Depression makes you feel down about yourself. The battle of depression is hard.

Fighting the highs and lows everyday. Those who deal with it stay strong and keep fighting.

You have turned for me my mourning into dancing; you have put off my sackcloth and clothed me with gladness, (Psalm 30:11 NKJV)

By Richie Sweitzer

Tribulation Of 2020

We all know that this pandemic is going on. With people dying every day. Not being able to see family in assisted living. That kills me inside every day. Having to put things we enjoy on hold. Feels like we are in a second great depression. With the whole world at a halt. The rate of depression is growing every day. This is affecting businesses big time. It is making paying bills even harder. Work for most people is totally different. The kids also have to suffer. There are no normal graduations. Things are different for the whole world.

And even as they did not like to retain God in their knowledge, God gave them over to a debased mind, to do those things which are not fitting (Romans 1:28 NKJ)

By Richie Sweitzer

Coming Home

Today you would be so proud of me. Seeing the young man, I have become. How I have turned my life around. I know you are up there cheering me on. Pat, I miss you so very much. The memories of you are priceless. You were always like family to me. I will always have you in my heart. Everyday I think about you. Just to hear you say, "I'm proud of you". In my heart I know you are. To see what I have overcome. RIP Pat.

So when this corruptible has put on incorruption, and this mortal has put on immortality, then shall be brought to pass the saying that is written; "Death is swallowed up in victory." (1 Corinthians 15:54 NKJV)

By Richie Sweitzer

The Season Of Believing

This is the season to reflect on your faith. When your faith is put to the test. The pandemic is really testing our faith. It is the lord's way to see how his people react. To those who are for Christ. Your faith will be rewarded. The savior was born to bring restoration to earth. So, we can reconnect with the father. The season of believing is about King Jesus. Remember that he loves you Merry Christmas.

But with out faith it is impossible to please him, for he who comes to God must believe that he is, and that he is rewarder of those who diligently seek him. (Hebrews 11: 6 NKJV)

By Richie Sweitzer

A New Day Has Come

This has been a rough year for all of us. There are better days to come ahead. The time for hope has come to the door. When the light starts to shine. The light of hope in Jesus our savior. We must keep the faith going strong. This is the time to call on his name. It is time for reflections on our actions. Hope is knocking at the door of your heart. Let the light of Jesus in your heart. We will come out of this together.

For I know the thoughts that I think toward you, Says the lord, thoughts of peace and not of evil, to give you a future and a hope. (Jeremiah 29:11 NKJV)

By Richie Sweitzer

Ocean Breeze

When the Holy Spirit enters a room there is still silence. We can feel his presence like a breeze. He is our teacher through this dark world. Through him we have hope and peace. The holy spirit lights up any empty void. Keep in mind the Holy Spirit is a person. Wherever you go the Holy Spirit is with you.

Now may the God of hope fill you with all joy and peace in believing, that you may abound in hope by the power of The Holy Spirit.

(Romans 15:13 NKJV)

By Richie Sweitzer

The One

You are the one who saves us from ourselves. He knows what we have been through. Jesus wants to take us out of the dark place. We must be open and let him in. My part is in the hands of Jesus. The future is possible by his blood. This goes for anyone who is in a dark place. We can always cry out to Jesus.

For you did not receive the spirit of bondage again to fear, but you received the spirit of adoption by whom we cry out, "abba, Father." (Romans 8:15 NKJV)

By Richie Sweitzer

My Sacrifice

The death on the cross was the best sacrifice. By his blood we die to ourselves. To live we must give up something. He teaches us how to sacrifice our time. This life is not ours. We are to show others how to sacrifice things. Love is the second-best sacrifice. This is a selfless act towards others. That is what the world needs to see more of.

Therefore we were buried with him through baptism into death, that just as Christ was raised from the dead by the glory of the father, even so we also should walk in the newness of life.(Romans 6:4 NKJV)

By Richie Sweitzer

Kingdoms

There are two kingdoms in this world. The first one is kingdom of light. That is where Jesus sits at. His name forever reigns till the end. Then there is the kingdom of darkness. This is where satan stands at. Satan reign is only for a short time. In the end Jesus reign will forever live. The enemy's reign will come to an end for good.

By Richie Sweitzer

Patterns

There are different patterns for each person. Everyone is born with a special pattern. These gifts we have are patterns. We are to use them for his glory. The glory is to build his kingdom. Many use it for their own self glory. That used to be me at one point in my life.

Every good gift and every perfect gift is from above, and comes down from the father of lights, with whom there is no variation or shadow of turning.

(James 1:17 NKJV)

By Richie Sweitzer

The Element Of Freedom

Salvation is the key to true freedom in life. Freedom brings a peace of mind to you. We are free through Jesus Christ. He is the key to salvation and life. That is what loosens us from the enemy grip. The enemy wants to keep us as his slave. Jesus is going to kick on him like a door mat.

Nor is there salvation in any other, for there is no other name under heaven given among men by which we must be saved."

(Acts 4:12 NKJV)

By Richie Sweitzer

Love Heals All

Love can take care of any issue you have. There is nothing too hard for her. She always has her arms open and ready. This is the one true friend you can count on. I know from personal experience what she can do. With her help I have overcome many obstacles. She is the best listener you can have. You just have to come as you are. All you must do is trust her.

By Richie Sweitzer

Fly

We can fly into the hands of our heavenly father. The heavenly father protects us from danger. No one can take us out of his hands. He loves us just as we are. You can give the father all your burdens. This is a worry-free zone. The father gives us a clear view on life. He always pulls the best out of us.

By Richie Sweitzer

Change Of Season

In life we go through different seasons. Some seasons are more challenging than others. My last season was definitely challenging for me. They are to help us grow in the faith. That is what strengthens are spiritual muscles.

The Lord puts us in certain seasons for a reason. We just have to trust in what he is doing.

To everything there is a season, and a time for every purpose under heaven: (Ecclesiastes 3:1 NKJV)

By Richie Sweitzer

Let Me Show You

Sometimes we need a reminder that things are ok. Lately I have been fighting myself. Grace tells us we are a loved child of God. The love that protects us from danger. He understands our story better then anyone else. Jesus knows the pain we go through every day.

By Richie Sweitzer

Power Of Hugs

There is something about the power of hugs. They can make a difference in someone's day. Hugs help build one's self-confidence. You can help your health through hugs. One hug can brighten your day. I believe that hugs can change a person's mood. Sometimes all someone needs a is a little love.

By Richie Sweitzer

Shining Down

You will always be my light guiding my path. No one loved me like you did great grandma. I loved you to the moon and back with all my heart. Great grandma you will forever be my light walking with me. You will be shining down forever in my heart. No one filled my heart with joy like you did.

There was no one else like you great grandma. You are my best friend cheering me on.

Then Jesus spoke to them again, saying "I am the light of the world. He who follows me shall not walk in darkness, but have the light of life."

(John 8:12 NKJV)

By Richie Sweitzer

Cruise

We all walk this journey called life. As we face the trials of wild desires. Life is like playing a game of chess. It takes strategic thinking in life. Cruising down the curbs and turns of life. Life may throw her curve balls at us. She wants to see us fail at are dreams. We are people who fight for dreams.

By Richie Sweitzer

Soldiers Of Faith

When engaging in a battlefield stand firm. The battlefield is the cruel world. We need to adapt in battle. You have to learn there weakness. We have to keep the faith strong. Jesus is our source of strength. Soldiers of faith fighting on there knees.

Now faith is the substance of things hoped for, the evidence of things not seen. (Hebrews 11:1 NKJV)

By Richie Sweitzer

Unspeakable peace

This kind of peace comes from on high. The peace breaks the separation between us. When Jesus broke the veil with the trinity. That peace is always present with us. The peace is with you during hardship. You can wrap her like a blanket. She is warm and gentle. Peace is like a mother with open arms.

For he himself is our peace, who has made both one and has broken down the middle wall of separation,(Ephesians 2:14 NKJV)

By Richie Sweitzer

Bleed The Same

Jesus died for everyone of us in this world. When this world is killing shooting for no reason. We all bleed the same. The world has there view of life all messed up. God created all men and woman equal. There is constant discrimination going on every-day. These people need there minds transformed from within. That comes through the transformation in Christ.

By Richie Sweitzer

Voice Of Truth

The voice of truth is like a breeze coming through. Gentle and understanding to comfort us. When you keep getting slammed with tribulation. That is when the voice of Jesus comes in. To hear Jesus say that I am with you. Lay down your heavy heart in my arms. The voice of truth says you don't have to fight this battle. You have a friend who always walks with you.

By Richie Sweitzer

Eagle Wings

We can soar like eagles with wings of faith.Flying through the clouds of hope. That any door can open for you. See what life has to offer us. Life shows us many different doors to take. Each door leads you down a different path. Take your faith down the road of life. The road of life has many twists and turns.

By Richie Sweitzer

Crash and Burn

When your heart is torn into pieces you want to shut out the world. Your heart has an unfilled void. It feels like everything around you are falling apart. Everything in your world is going in a downward spiral. Deep down inside you want to break out. You crash and burn into a dark place. Then an angel comes at the right time. The whole time somebody been watching over you.

By Richie Sweitzer

Character

Someone character says a lot about them. Character shows a person type of leadership. It shows what kind of fruit they produce. I have been down the road of bad character. Character is like the fruit you pick. They can be bitter or sweet. What are your leadership skills like? Good character makes a great leader.

Do not be deceived "bad company ruins good morals." (1 Corinthians 15:33 NKJV)

By Richie Sweitzer

Right Here

I will forever be in your hearts always. You are like a flower in my heart. My flower of comfort and strength. Those dark empty days will be filled with joy. When the broken heart finds inner hope. See the rainbow in the sky of love. Knowing that you are always loved all the time. Always knowing his presence is around us.

By Richie Sweitzer

Every Time

When you feel all alone deep inside. All your heart feels heavy sadness. Some days you want to block out the world. It does not help when people want to keep you down. When it feels like everything is falling apart. You gave nothing but all your time. The world expects you to just keep going on like nothing happened.

By Richie Sweitzer

Don't Matter

People will talk about you regardless. There were people who doubted me during my journey. That did not stop me from getting help. It does not matter what people say about you. You have the advantage of proving them wrong. When negativity comes, turn it to a positive.

By Richie Sweitzer

From This Moment On

From this moment on I will stand tall on my feet. I will not be walked on like a doormat. You can keep that drama outside the door. My feelings is nobodys playground. Never let anybody say you're not important. So don't be afraid to speak up for yourself. Trust me, I know the feeling.

Don't let your hearts be troubled. Trust in God, and trust also in me. (John 14:1 NKJV)

By Richie Sweitzer

Gratitude

Have appreciation for what you do have. Being grateful for all the small things. Showing a little respect for those we care about. WE have plenty to be thankful for, like family, friends, shelter. Sometimes we forget what really matters. The things we take for granted is what really matters. So, lets enjoy the things we have.

Oh. Give thanks to the lord, for He is good! his mercy endures forever. (Psalm 106:1 NKJV)

By Richie Sweitzer

Let The Sun Rise

When the days look grey and gloomy. It feels like no one cares about what you think. You have someone who always listens to you. This person loves you for who you are. He is the light during your dark days. The light has helped me through many days.

By Richie Sweitzer

Come Together

We need to come together with a peaceful sulotion for these shootings. The are too many lives being taken daily. All these shootings and hate must come to a hualt. This hate only spreads like a dangerous virus.It affects the heart like a deadly poison. WE must come as a nation with love.

This world needs a lot more love in it. The cure to the problem in the world is love.

By Richie Sweitzer

Kingdom Minds

Thinking with a Christ like mindset in motion. He models the way we should think and act. The road was already carved out for us. It is up to us if we follow that road. What road are you going down in life. There are only 2 roads to follow in life. The kingdom road leads to life. Then the worlds road leads to death.

By Richie Sweitzer

9 798990 490727